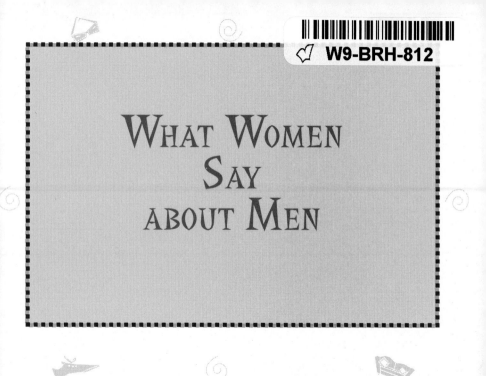

WHAT WOMEN
SAY
ABOUT MEN

WHAT WOMEN SAY ABOUT MEN

Witty Observations on the Male of the Species

Edited by Mary G. Rodarte

Ariel Books

Andrews McMeel Publishing

Kansas City

02 03 04 05 06 BIN 10 9 8 7 6 5 4 3 2 1

Jacket illustration © 2002 by Lisa Parett

ISBN: 0-7407-2238-7

Library of Congress Control Card Number: 2001095903

WHAT WOMEN
SAY
ABOUT MEN

CONTENTS

INTRODUCTION

Every woman has a different story to tell, but the theme is almost always the same: What's up with men? We are surrounded by them—brothers, boyfriends, uncles, husbands, friends, fathers, coworkers, neighbors—but trying to figure them out is about as easy as figuring out the meaning of life.

Throughout history, the two sexes have misunderstood each other. This fact is a source of comfort to some (it's *always* been "us" against "them") and a cause of puzzlement to others (we are, after all, the same species, aren't we?). The

9

women quoted in this book are from all walks of life—authors, actresses, scientists, homemakers, journalists, artists—and each observes men from her unique perspective. But no matter how personal the feelings behind the pointed barbs or candid remarks, the truth in their words is universal: We may have to live side by side with men, but sometimes there is just no understanding them!

MEN SCHMEN

I regard men as a pleasant pastime but no more dependable than the British weather.

—Anna Raeburn

One hell of an outlay for a very small return with most of them.

—Glenda Jackson

Men are like a deck of cards. You'll find the occasional king, but most are jacks.

—Laura Swenson

Men and women, women and men. It will never work.

—Erica Jong

I no longer have the fear of being alone. It's cool to find out that you don't need a boyfriend to be happy.

—Drew Barrymore

No one should have to dance backwards all their lives.

—Jill Ruckelshaus

I don't have buried anger against men. Because my anger is right on the surface.

—Camille Paglia

*S*ome of my best leading men have been dogs and horses.

—Elizabeth Taylor

You have to be very fond of men. Very, very fond. You have to be very fond of them to love them. Otherwise they're simply unbearable.

—Marguerite Duras

Getting along with men isn't what's truly important. The vital knowledge is how to get along with a man. One man.

—Phyllis McGinley

Don't accept rides from strange men, and remember that all men are strange.

—Robin Morgan

Let us love dogs, let us only love dogs! Men and cats are unworthy creatures.

—Marie Bashkirtseff

The ceiling isn't glass; it's a very dense layer of men.

—Anne Jardim

Men, being conditioned badly, are always feeling nooses closing around their necks, even dumpy boors no girl would take on a bet.

—Cynthia Heimel

How wrong it is for a woman to expect the man to build the world she wants, rather than set out to create it herself.

—Anaïs Nin

Can you imagine a world without men? No crime and lots of happy . . . women.

—Nicole Hollander

What a commentary on our civilization, when being alone is considered suspect; when one has to apologize for it, make excuses, hide the fact that one practices it—like a secret vice!

—Anne Morrow Lindbergh

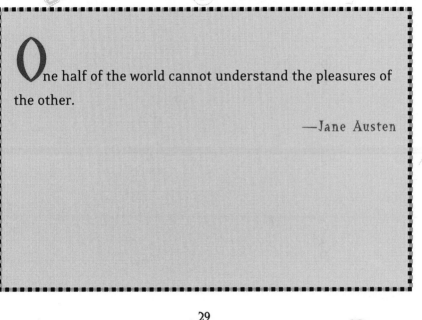

One half of the world cannot understand the pleasures of the other.

—Jane Austen

The best way to mend a broken heart is time and girlfriends.

—Gwyneth Paltrow

We are becoming the men we wanted to marry.

—Gloria Steinem

Women are not men's equals in anything except responsibility. We are not their inferiors, either, or even their superiors. We are quite simply different races.

—Phyllis McGinley

A woman without a man is like a fish without a bicycle.

—Irina Dunn

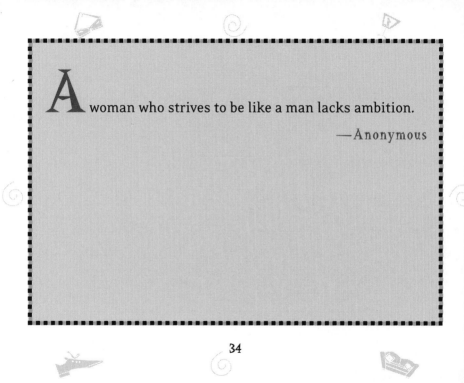

A woman who strives to be like a man lacks ambition.

—Anonymous

In our family we don't divorce our men—we bury them.

—Ruth Gordon

The more I see of men, the more I like dogs.

—Madame de Staël

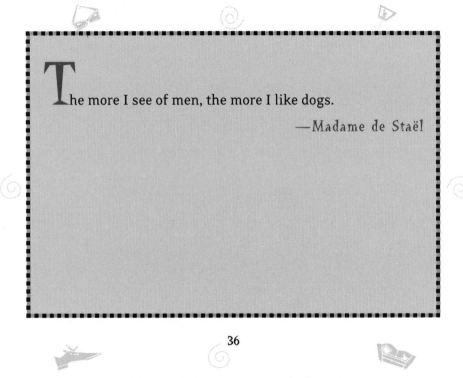

I don't need a man to rectify my existence. The most profound relationship we'll ever have is the one with ourselves.

—Shirley MacLaine

Sometimes I wonder if men and women really suit each other. Perhaps they should live next door and just visit now and then.

—Katharine Hepburn

It's a man's world, and you men can have it.

—Katherine Anne Porter

I learned that women were smart and capable, could live in community together without men, and in fact did not need men much.

—Anna Quindlen

If you want anything said, ask a man. If you want anything done, ask a woman.

—Margaret Thatcher

I didn't want to be a boy, ever, but I was outraged that his height and intelligence were graces for him and gaucheries for me.

—Jane Rule

The time you spend grieving over a man should never exceed the amount of time you actually spent with him.

—Rita Rudner

If the right man does not come along, there are many fates far worse. One is to have the wrong man come along.

—Letitia Baldrige

To Honor and Obey? No Way!

I think, therefore I'm single.

—Liz Winston

I, like most mothers, would kill for my children. With a husband, it would depend on the mood I was in.

—Carly Simon

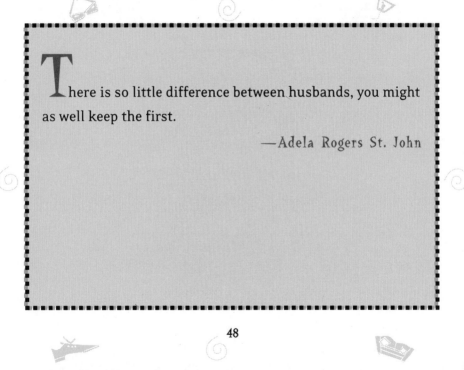

There is so little difference between husbands, you might as well keep the first.

—Adela Rogers St. John

I have no wish for a second husband. I had enough of the first. I like to have my own way—to lie down mistress, and get up master.

—Susanna Moodie

It is one thing to enjoy a man's society for an hour or two now and then, and another to annex him permanently.... The worst trial I ever had to endure ... was having a husband continually on my hands.

—Gertrude Atherton

It was so cold I almost got married.

—Shelley Winters

Any gal is gonna go out of her mind when she looks at her husband one day and realizes that she is not living with a man any longer. She is living with a reclining chair that burps.

—Roseanne Arnold

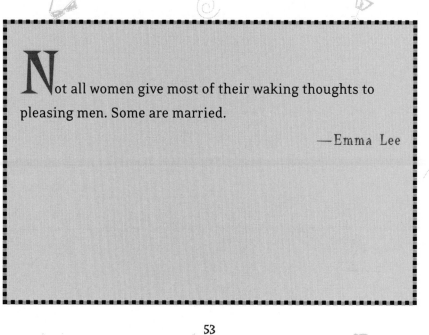

Not all women give most of their waking thoughts to pleasing men. Some are married.

—Emma Lee

It seemed to me that the desire to get married—which, I regret to say, I believe is basic and primal in women—is followed almost immediately by an equally basic and primal urge—which is to be single again.

—Nora Ephron

Marrying a man is like buying something you've been admiring for a long time in a shop window. You may love it when you get it home, but it doesn't always go with everything else.

—Jean Kerr

When two people marry, they become in the eyes of the law one person, and that person is the husband.

—Shana Alexander

Men are nicer to the women they don't marry.

—Belle Livingston

Whenever I date a guy, I think, is this the man I want my children to spend their weekends with?

—Rita Rudner

We all marry strangers. All men are strangers to all women.

—Mary Heaton Vorse

Before marriage a man will lay awake all night thinking about something you said; after marriage, he'll fall asleep before you finish saying it.

—Helen Rowland

The trouble with some women is that they get all excited about nothing—and then marry him.

—Cher

Whenever you want to marry someone, go have lunch with his ex-wife.

—Shelley Winters

If love means never having to say you're sorry, then marriage means always having to say everything twice. Husbands, due to an unknown quirk of the universe, never hear you the first time.

—Estelle Getty

I never married because I have three pets at home that answer the same purpose as a husband. I have a dog that growls every morning, a parrot that swears all afternoon, and a cat that comes home late at night.

—Marie Corelli

An archaeologist is the best husband a woman can have. The older she gets, the more interested he is in her.

—Agatha Christie

I wasn't allowed to speak while my husband was alive, and since he's gone no one has been able to shut me up.

—Hedda Hopper

I've given my memoirs far more thought than any of my marriages. You can't divorce a book.

—Gloria Swanson

Estimated from a wife's experience, the average man spends fully one-quarter of his life in looking for his shoes.

—Helen Rowland

I have yet to hear a man ask for advice on how to combine marriage and a career.

—Gloria Steinem

I married beneath me, all women do.

—Nancy Astor

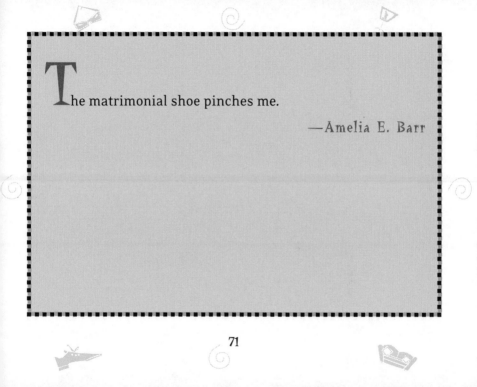

The matrimonial shoe pinches me.

—Amelia E. Barr

As far as I am concerned I would rather spend the rest of my life in prison than marry again.

—George Sand

O, girls! set your affections on cats, poodles, parrots or lap-dogs; but let matrimony alone.

—Fanny Fern

Any intelligent woman who reads the marriage contract, and then goes into it, deserves all the consequences.

—Isadora Duncan

When you see what some girls marry, you realize how they must hate to work for a living.

—Helen Rowland

would rather be a beggar and single than a queen and married.

—Elizabeth I

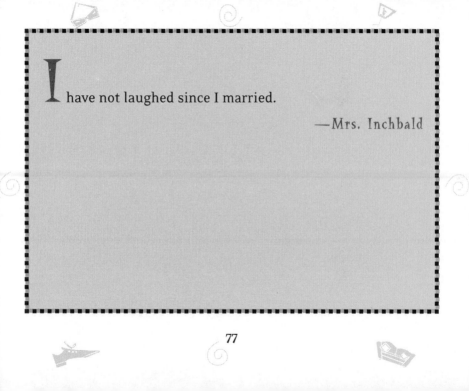

I have not laughed since I married.

—Mrs. Inchbald

Those wishing to enter the marriage state had better not come to me for advice, for I disapprove of it altogether.

—Charlotte-Elisabeth, Duchesse d'Orléans

It is always incomprehensible to a man that a woman should ever refuse an offer of marriage.

—Jane Austen

The only way to make a husband over according to one's ideas . . . would be to adopt him at an early age, say four.

—Mary Roberts Rinehart

Don't marry a man to reform him—that's what reform schools are for.

—Mae West

Bigamy is having one husband too many. Monogamy is the same.

—Erica Jong

My husband will never chase another woman. He's too fine, too decent, too old.

—Gracie Allen

The guy who used to appear at your front door every night because he was wild to see you, now appears there every night because that's where he happens to live.

—Lucille Kallen

I want to be more than a rose in my husband's lapel.

—Margaret Trudeau

A girl must marry for love, and keep on marrying until she finds it.

—Zsa Zsa Gabor

Personally, I think if a woman hasn't met the right man by the time she's twenty-four, she may be lucky.

—Deborah Kerr

It is better to know as little as possible of the defects of the person with whom you are to pass your life.

—Jane Austen

An easy-going husband is the one indispensable comfort of life.

—Ouida

My husband said he wanted to have a relationship with a redhead, so I dyed my hair red.

—Jane Fonda

Brought up to respect the conventions, love had to end in marriage. I'm afraid it did.

—Bette Davis

Women have one great advantage over men. It is commonly thought that if they marry they have done enough, and need career no further. If a man marries, on the other hand, public opinion is all against him if he takes this view.

—Rose Macaulay

Next to hot chicken soup, a tattoo of an anchor on your chest, and penicillin, I consider a honeymoon one of the most overrated events in the world.

—Erma Bombeck

Oh! how I long to see my dear husband, that I may quarrel with him!

—Mrs. Inchbald

Do not think about trying to make it through a lifetime with a man. Just concentrate on making it through a year. . . . The reason a man will not try to split up with you after a year or so is his limitless fear of breaking in a new model.

—Stephanie Brush

Trust you husband, adore your husband, and get as much as you can in your own name.

—Joan Rivers

Never marry a man who can't please you.

—Dr. Joyce Brothers

... *I*f a woman *doubts* as to whether she should accept a man or not, she certainly ought to refuse him. If she can hesitate as to "Yes," she ought to say "No," directly.

—Jane Austen

So that ends my first experience of matrimony, which I always thought a highly over-rated performance.

—Isadora Duncan

Marriage could be the greatest success in the sociological history of humanity if the man would or could play fair. But, I believe any woman with independent instincts, with the dream of making her individual personality count for something in the world, might just as well shun marriage.

—Maud Gonne

Any one must see at a glance that if men and women marry those whom they do not love, they must love those whom they do not marry.

—Harriet Martineau

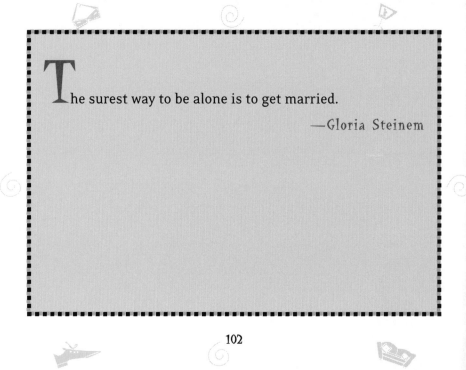

The surest way to be alone is to get married.

—Gloria Steinem

And I knew that in spite of all the roses and kisses and restaurant dinners a man showered on a woman before he married her, what he secretly wanted when the wedding ended was for her to flatten out underneath his feet like Mrs. Willard's kitchen mat.

—Sylvia Plath

Oh, what a pother ... women make about marriage! ... Safeguarded, kept in the dark, hinted at, segregated, repressed, all so that at a given moment they may be delivered or may deliver their daughters over, to minister to a man?

—Vita Sackville-West

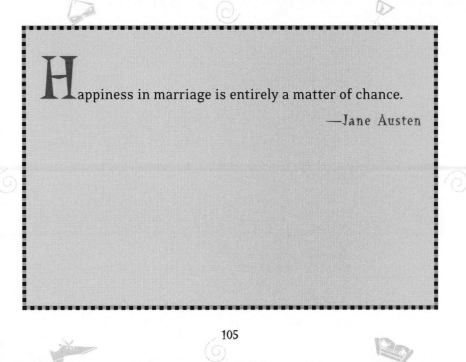

Happiness in marriage is entirely a matter of chance.

—Jane Austen

Personally I know nothing about sex because I've always been married.

—Zsa Zsa Gabor

Other things titillate me more keenly than the pale pleasures of marriage.

—Christina, Queen of Sweden

If you ain't got on to it by now, that I'm no little, tremblin' wife, you never will. Those kind has nerves. I only got nerve.

—Julie M. Lippmann

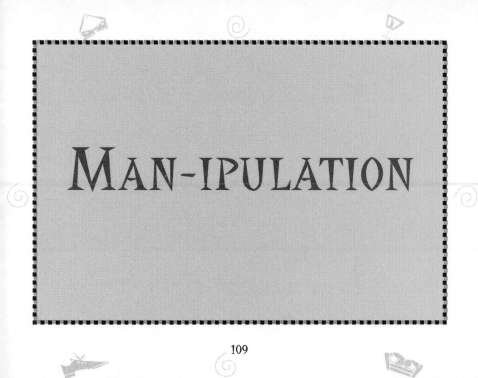

MAN-IPULATION

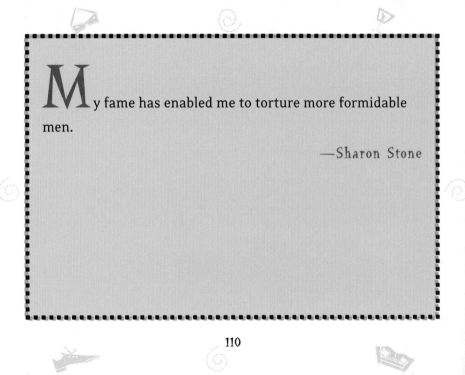

My fame has enabled me to torture more formidable men.

—Sharon Stone

The male is a domestic animal, which, if treated with firmness and kindness, can be trained to do most things.

—Jilly Cooper

The only thing worse than a man you can't control is a man you can.

—Margo Kaufman

Beware of men who cry. It's true that men who cry are sensitive and in touch with feelings, but the only feelings they tend to be sensitive to and in touch with are their own.

—Nora Ephron

If you have trouble attracting men, try ordering pizza instead. This way you can get whatever you like—the right size, the right toppings, and once the delivery boy is in your house, he's yours.

—Hilary Dalton

I never understood women's liberation. I always got what I wanted from men without asking.

—Martha Graham

Learn to use men without surrendering to them. Have confidence in those who, if necessary, are courageous enough to contradict you.

—Catherine the Great

[M]en] are like street cars, another comes along every fifteen minutes, the trick is not to let one run over you.

—Frances Deck

When you are in love with someone you want to be near him all the time, except when you are out buying things and charging them to him.

—Miss Piggy

I want a man who's kind and understanding. Is that too much to ask of a millionaire?

—Zsa Zsa Gabor

The best way to get most husbands to do something is to suggest that perhaps they're too old to do it.

—Shirley MacLaine

You know how I end relationships . . . ? I don't say, "This isn't working out." Or, "I don't want to see you anymore." This is a tip to remember, girls. If I never want to see a man again, I just say, "You know, I love you. . . . I want to marry you. . . . I want to have your children. . . ." Sometimes they make skid marks.

—Rita Rudner

Most women set out to try to change a man, and when they have changed him they do not like him.

—Marlene Dietrich

The best way to find out if a man has done something is to advise him to do it. He will not be able to resist boasting that he has done it without being advised.

—Comtesse Diane

When a man wants to deceive you, he'll find a way of escape through the tiniest holes.

—Colette

So long as women are slaves, men will be knaves.

—Elizabeth Cady Stanton

Ever since Eve gave Adam the apple, there has been a misunderstanding between the sexes about gifts.

—Nan Robertson

It takes a woman twenty years to make a man of her son, and another woman twenty minutes to make a fool of him.

—Helen Rowland

I have honorable intentions towards no man.

—Maxine Elliott

Women's chains have been forged by men, not by anatomy.

—Estelle Ramey

A fox is a wolf who sends flowers.

—Ruth Weston

Gentlemen prefer doormats.

—Ruth Herschberger

Most men are reasonably useful in a crisis. The difficulty lies in convincing them that the situation has reached a critical point.

—Elizabeth Peters

I ask no favors for my sex. . . . All I ask of our brethren is that they will take their feet from off our necks.

—Sarah Moore Grimké

Beware of the man who praises women's liberation; he is about to quit his job.

—Erica Jong

Any woman can fool a man if she wants to and if he's in love with her.

—Agatha Christie

Never go to bed mad. Stay up and fight.

—Phyllis Diller

Remember all Men would be tyrants if they could.

—Abigail Adams

When men talk about defense, they always claim to be protecting women and children, but they never ask the women and children what they think.

—Pat Schroeder

I am a marvelous housekeeper. Every time I leave a man I keep his house.

—Zsa Zsa Gabor

Be fond of the man who jests at his scars, if you like; but never believe he is being on the level with you.

—Pamela Hansford Johnson

From my experience of life I believe my personal motto should be "Beware of men bearing flowers."

—Muriel Spark

I never liked the men I loved, and I never loved the men I liked.

—Fanny Brice

BOYS WILL BE BOYS

Boys frustrate me. I hate all their indirect messages, I hate game playing. Do you like me or don't you? Just tell me so I can get over you.

—Kirsten Dunst

The old myths had it wrong; woman was really created first, and in her need to mother she asked for a child. The Creator then gave her man . . .

—Anne Shannon Monroe

145

Whatever happened to the strong, silent type? Today's man talks, talks, talks 'til we're blue in the face. And I fear there's no undoing the damage. The new old saying? Boys will be noise.

—Nina Malkin

Maleness is wonderful, really, isn't it, honey? Perfect denial of reality.

—Erica Jong

What I expect from my male friends is that they are polite and clean.

—Anna Quindlen

It's just as hard for man to break the habit of thinking of himself as central to the species as it was to break the habit of thinking of himself as central to the universe.

—Elaine Morgan

No one is more arrogant toward women, more aggressive or scornful, than the man who is anxious about his virility.

—Simone de Beauvoir

The male ego with few exceptions is elephantine to start with.

—Bette Davis

A man is one who loses his illusions first, his teeth second, and his follies last.

—Helen Rowland

We had a lot in common. I loved him and he loved him.

—Shelley Winters

Because men are simple, they are not physically capable of handling more than one task at a time. Women can easily cook dinner, feed the baby, and talk on the phone all at once. Were a man to try this, he would probably explode.

—Roseanne Arnold

The standard Western adult male is rendered incapable of being comfortable with emotional expression ... being quite incapable of understanding what it is like to be someone else.

—Janet Daley

I have always thought that the difference between a man and a mule is that a mule could change his mind.

—Abigail Duniway

M en are always ready to respect anything that bores them.

—Marilyn Monroe

The usual masculine disillusionment is in discovering that a woman has a brain.

—Margaret Mitchell

I blame Rousseau, myself. "Man is born free," indeed. Man is not born free, he is born attached to his mother by a cord and is not capable of looking after himself for at least seven years (seventy in some cases).

—Katharine Whitehorn

If a man watches three football games in a row, he should be declared legally dead.

—Erma Bombeck

Woman: the peg on which the wit hangs his jest, the preacher his text, the cynic his grouch and the sinner his justification.

—Helen Rowland

Men weren't really the enemy—they were fellow victims suffering from an outmoded masculine mystique that made them feel unnecessarily inadequate when there were no bears to kill.

—Betty Friedan

I suppose when they reach a certain age some men are afraid to grow up. It seems the older the men get, the younger their new wives get.

—Elizabeth Taylor

In passing, also, I would like to say that the first time Adam had a chance he laid the blame on woman.

—Nancy Astor

A man's home may seem to be his castle on the outside; inside it is more often his nursery.

—Clare Boothe Luce

A man never knows how to say good-bye; a woman never knows when to say it.

—Helen Rowland

We do not ask man to represent us; it is hard enough in times like these for man to carry backbone enough to represent himself.

—Elizabeth Cady Stanton

Women want a family life that glitters and is stable. They don't want some lump spouse watching ice hockey in the late hours of his eighteenth beer.... They want, just like men, fun, love, fame, money, and power. And equal pay for equal work.

—Carolyn See

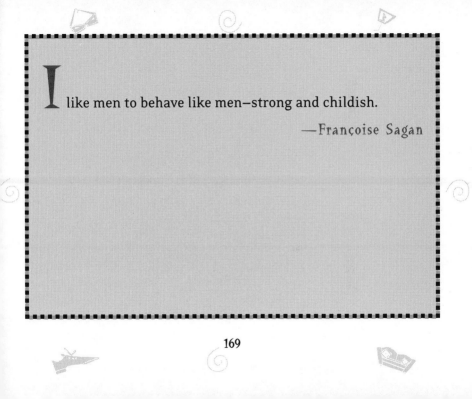

I like men to behave like men—strong and childish.

—Françoise Sagan

169

Men are too emotional to vote. Their conduct at baseball games and political conventions shows this, while their innate tendency to appeal to force renders them particularly unfit for the task of government.... Men's place is in the armory.

—Alice Duer Miller

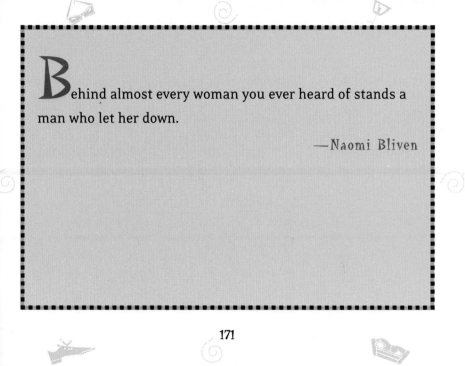

Behind almost every woman you ever heard of stands a man who let her down.

—Naomi Bliven

Giving a man space is like giving a dog a computer. The chances are he will not use it wisely.

—Bette-Jane Raphael

Macho does not prove mucho.

—Zsa Zsa Gabor

I refuse to consign the whole male sex to the nursery. I insist on believing that some men are my equals.

—Brigid Brophy

The reason some men fear older women is they fear their own mortality.

—Frances Lear

I've been married to one Marxist and one Fascist, and neither one would take the garbage out.

—Lee Grant

Men play harder than they work; women work harder than they play.

—Mary Roberts Rinehart

If a woman gets nervous, she'll eat or go shopping. A man will attack a country—it's a whole other way of thinking.

—Elayne Boosler

Women have served all these centuries as looking-glasses possessing the magic and delicious power of reflecting the figure of man at twice its natural size.

—Virginia Woolf

Men often marry their mothers.

—Edna Ferber

I'd like somebody to breed a male, genus homo, who could go and fetch a twelve-inch by eight-inch black suède purse lying in the middle of a white bedspread and not come back looking baffled and saying he couldn't find it.

—Margaret Halsey

Men don't live well by themselves. They don't even live like people. They live like bears with furniture.

—Rita Rudner

The only time a woman really succeeds in changing a man is when he is a baby.

—Natalie Wood

Testosterone does not have to be toxic.

—Anna Quindlen

Women speak because they wish to speak; whereas, a man speaks only when driven to speech by something outside himself—like, for instance, he can't find any clean socks.

—Jean Kerr

There are really no men at all. There are grown-up boys, and middle-aged boys, and elderly boys.

—Mary Roberts Rinehart

My ancestors wandered lost in the wilderness for forty years because even in biblical times, men would not stop to ask for directions.

—Elayne Boosler

If you talk about yourself, he'll think you're boring. If you talk about others, he'll think you're a gossip. If you talk about him, he'll think you're a brilliant conversationalist.

—Linda Sunshine

When a man talks to you about his mother's cooking, pay no attention, for between the ages of twelve and twenty-one, a boy can eat large quantities of anything and never feel it.

—Sarah Tyson Rorer

As long as you know most men are like children, you know everything.

—Coco Chanel

190

PILLOW TALK

Women's virtue is man's greatest invention.

—Cornelia Otis Skinner

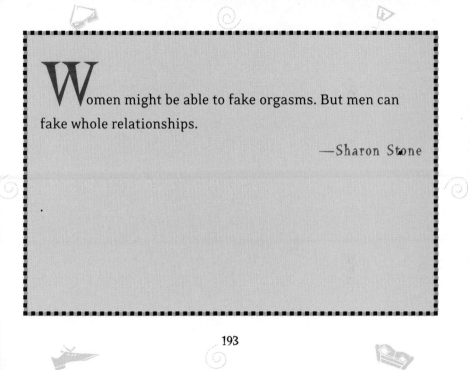

Women might be able to fake orgasms. But men can fake whole relationships.

—Sharon Stone

193

Men would always rather be made love to than talked to.

—Dorothy M. Richardson

Anyone who's a great kisser I'm always interested in.

—Cher

... **t**hose creatures with two legs and eight hands.

—Jayne Mansfield

A man's heart may have a secret sanctuary where only one woman may enter, but it is full of little anterooms which are seldom vacant.

—Helen Rowland

I don't know why women want any of the things men have when one of the things that women have is men.

—Coco Chanel

198

People who are so dreadfully devoted to their wives are so apt, from mere habit, to get devoted to other people's wives as well.

—Jane Welsh Carlyle

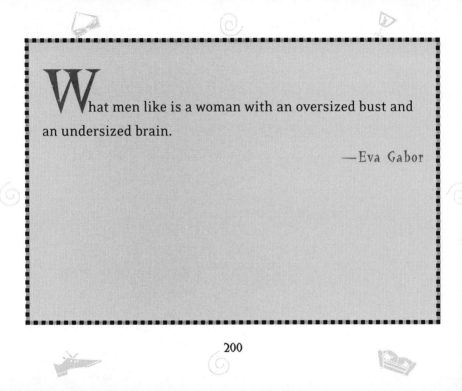

What men like is a woman with an oversized bust and an undersized brain.

—Eva Gabor

It isn't that gentlemen really prefer blondes, it's just that we look dumber.

—Anita Loos

Expiring for love is beautiful but stupid.

—Jenny Holzer

It's not the men in my life that counts, it's the life in my men.

—Mae West

Dr. Ruth says we women should tell our lovers how to make love to us. My boyfriend goes nuts if I tell him how to drive!

—Pam Stone

Men, since they made gods in their own image, feel that their bodies are essentially all right. Studies show that while women unrealistically distort their bodies negatively, men unrealistically distort theirs positively.

—Naomi Wolf

Husbands are like fires. They go out when unattended.

—Zsa Zsa Gabor

Love is the whole history of a woman's life, but it is an episode in a man's.

—Madame de Staël

A man in the house is worth two in the street.

—Mae West

... **b**ecause men admire muscle and physical force, they assume that we do too.

—Elizabeth Gould Davis

I'm glad I'm a woman because I don't have to worry about getting men pregnant.

—Nell Dunn

These are very confusing times. For the first time in history a woman is expected to combine: intelligence with a sharp hairdo, a raised consciousness with high heels, and an open, nonsexist relationship with a tan guy who has a great bod.

—Lynda Barry

He was every other inch a gentleman.

—Rebecca West

It is possible that blondes also prefer gentlemen.

—Mamie Van Doren

A girl can wait for the right man to come along but in the meantime that still doesn't mean she can't have a wonderful time with all the wrong ones.

—Cher

When he's late for dinner, I know he's either having an affair or is lying dead in the street. I always hope it's the street.

—Jessica Tandy

One of the advantages of living alone is that you don't have to wake up in the arms of a loved one.

—Marion Smith

What is man's part in sex but a perpetual waving of flags and blowing of trumpets and avoidance of the fighting?

—Dora Russell

Men make love more intensely at twenty, but make love better, however, at thirty.

—Catherine II of Russia

218

A woman who has known but one man is like a person who has heard only one composer.

—Isadora Duncan

I like to wake up each morning feeling a new man.

—Jean Harlow

Agentleman is a patient wolf.

—Henriett Tiarks

No man can be held throughout the day by what happens throughout the night.

—Sally Stanford

Plain women know more about men than beautiful ones do.

—Katharine Hepburn

The average man is more interested in a woman who is interested in him than he is in a woman—any woman—with beautiful legs.

—Marlene Dietrich

A woman has got to love a bad man once or twice in her life to be thankful for a good one.

—Marjorie Kinnan Rawlings

When women go wrong, men go right after them.

—Mae West

The compulsion to find a lover and husband in a single person has doomed more women to misery than any other illusion.

—Carolyn Heilbrun

*S*ome men are so macho they'll get you pregnant just to kill a rabbit.

—Maureen Murphy

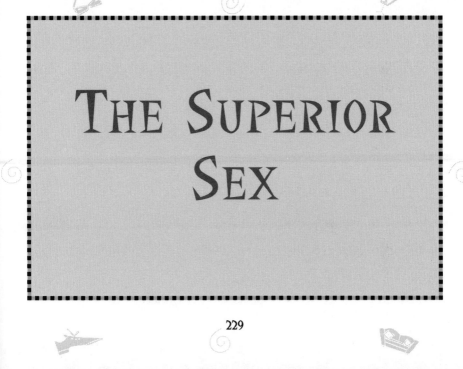

THE SUPERIOR SEX

God made man, and then said I can do better than that and made woman.

—Adela Rogers St. John

Men should only be the accessories of the strong woman.

—Marie Bashkirtseff

There aren't any hard women, only soft men.

—Raquel Welch

Behind every great man there is a surprised woman.

—Maryon Pearson

Men may have discovered fire, but women discovered how to play with it.

—Sarah Jessica Parker

The men are much alarmed by certain speculations about women; and well they may be, for when the horse and ass begin to think and argue, adieu to riding and driving.

—Adelaide Anne Procter

Men don't like independent women.

—Shirley Chisholm

One cannot be always laughing at a man without now and then stumbling on something witty.

—Jane Austen

I could have succeeded much easier in my career had I been a man.

—Henrietta Green

A broken heart is what makes life so wonderful five years later, when you see the guy in an elevator and he is fat and smoking a cigar and saying long-time-no-see. If he hadn't broken your heart, you couldn't have that glorious feeling of relief!

—Phyllis Battelle

Women want mediocre men, and men are working hard to be as mediocre as possible.

—Margaret Mead

The art of being a woman can never consist of being a bad imitation of a man.

—Olga Knopf

Men are very strange. When they wake up they want breakfast. They don't eat candy in the morning like we do. They want things like toast. I don't have these recipes.

—Elayne Boosler

I require only three things of a man. He must be handsome, ruthless, and stupid.

—Dorothy Parker

... It seems to me highly improbable that women are going to realize their human potential without alienating men—some men, anyway.

—Elizabeth Janeway

Boyfriends weren't friends at all; they were prizes, escorts, symbols of achievement, fascinating strangers, the Other.

—Susan Allen Toth

That seems to be the haunting fear of mankind—that the advancement of women will sometime, someway, someplace, interfere with some man's comfort.

—Nellie L. McClung

One of the things being in politics has taught me is that men are not a reasoned or reasonable sex.

—Margaret Thatcher

If men can run the world, why can't they stop wearing neckties? How intelligent is it to start the day by tying a little noose around your neck?

—Linda Ellerbee

Whatever women do they must do twice as well to be thought of as half as good. Luckily, this is not difficult.

—Charlotte Whitton

Men are not amusing during the shooting season; but, after all . . . men were not especially designed to amuse women.

—Gertrude Atherton

A woman needs to know but one man well to understand all men; whereas, a man may know all women and not understand one of them.

—Helen Rowland

But oh, what a woman I should be if an able young man would consecrate his life to me as secretaries and technicians do to their men employers.

—Mable Ulrich

If women ruled the world and we all got massages, there would be no war.

—Carrie Snow

I have always wanted to be a man, if only for the reason that I would like to have gauged the value of my intellect.

—Margot Asquith

My idea of a screamingly boring man is a chap who doesn't like the company of women.

—Anne Edwards

The evidence indicates that woman is, on the whole, biologically superior to man.

—Ashley Montagu

Women in America too easily accept the idea of their inferiority to men—if not actually, then in order to curry favor with men, who imagine it easier to live with inferiors than with equals.

—Pearl S. Buck

I would even go to Washington . . . just to glimpse Jane Q. Public being sworn as the first female president of the United States, while her husband holds the Bible and wears a silly pillbox hat and matching coat.

—Anna Quindlen

[W]omen want] the seemingly impossible: that men treat them with the respect and fairmindedness with which they treat most men.

—Joyce Carol Oates

What this woman wants, with all due respect to S. Freud, is for men to stop asking that question and to realize that women are human beings, not some alien species. They want the same things men want.

—Diane White

When someone's saying "I love you," he always ought to give a lot of details: Like, Why does he love you? And, How much does he love you? And, When and where did he first begin to love you? Favorable comparisons with all the other women he ever loved are also welcome. And even though he insists it would take forever to count the ways in which he loves you, let him start counting.

—Judith Viorst

Women share with men the need for personal success, even the taste for power, and no longer are we willing to satisfy those needs through the achievements of surrogates, whether husbands, children, or merely role models.

—Elizabeth Dole

Women must learn not to be subservient to the wishes of their fathers, husbands and partners, because then they do not fulfill their own ambitions.

—Petra Kelly

Women have been the truly active people in all cultures, without whom human society would long ago have perished, though our activity has most often been on the behalf of men and children.

—Adrienne Rich

We bear the world and we make it. . . . There was never a great man who had not a great mother.

—Olive Schreiner

When he said we were trying to make a fool of him, I could only murmur that the Creator had beat us to it.

—Ilka Chase

266

The classic function of the "warrior" helped men throughout history achieve a sense of confidence they needed to cope with women.

—Page Smith

Men talk about what happened; women talk about what really happened. Men talk about what they are supposed to talk about; women talk about what really concerns them.

—Tina Brown

Why are women so much more interesting to men than men are to women?

—Virginia Woolf

If it wasn't for women, men would still be hanging from trees.

—Marilyn Peterson

I am a woman meant for a man, but I never found a man who could compete.

—Bette Davis

Book design and composition
by Diane Hobbing
of Snap-Haus Graphics
in Dumont, NJ